MARCILLINUS ASOGWA

Justice's Redemption: Imaginary Battles for Right

First edition

This book was professionally typeset on Reedsy.
Find out more at reedsy.com

Contents

1

The Fall of Justice

The sun hung low on the horizon, casting long shadows over the picturesque town of Justice. Its cobblestone streets were lined with quaint cottages adorned with colorful flowers, and the air was filled with the laughter of children playing in the town square. But beneath the surface of this idyllic facade lurked a darkness that threatened to engulf the entire town.

At the heart of Justice stood the imposing figure of Mayor Ethan Blackwood, a man whose iron grip on the town's affairs was matched only by his insatiable thirst for power. From his ornate office in the town hall, he ruled over Justice with an iron fist, brooking no dissent and tolerating no opposition.

But on this fateful day, Mayor Blackwood's reign was about to be challenged in ways he could never have imagined.

As the sun dipped below the horizon, casting the town in an eerie twilight, a hush fell over the streets of Justice. The residents, going about their evening routines, were unaware of the storm clouds gathering on the horizon.

In the town square, a small crowd had gathered, drawn by the sound of raised voices and the sight of flashing lights. Pushing their way through the throng, they came upon a scene of chaos and confusion. A fire raged in the center of the square, sending plumes of black smoke billowing into the sky. The flames licked hungrily at the surrounding buildings, threatening to consume everything in their path.

Panic spread like wildfire through the crowd as people scrambled to escape the inferno. But amidst the chaos, a lone figure stood silhouetted against the flames, a look of grim determination etched upon their face.

It was Sarah Thompson, a young woman with fiery red hair and a fierce spirit to match. As the daughter of one of Justice's most prominent families, she had always chafed against the suffocating constraints of small-town life. But now, as she faced down the raging fire threatening to destroy everything she held dear, she knew that she was the only one who could save Justice from the darkness that threatened to engulf it.

With a steely resolve, Sarah plunged into the inferno, heedless of the danger that surrounded her. The heat was intense, searing her skin and singeing her hair, but she pressed on, driven by a sense of duty and a desire to protect her home.

As she battled the flames, a shadowy figure watched from the shadows, their eyes glittering with malice. They knew that Sarah posed a threat to their plans, and they would stop at nothing to see her defeated.

And so, as the fire raged on into the night, the fate of Justice hung in the balance, teetering on the edge of oblivion. Little did the townsfolk know that this was only the beginning of a battle that would test their courage, their loyalty, and their very humanity.

2

Whispers in the Dark

The morning sun rose over Justice, casting a golden glow over the town's rooftops and alleys. But despite the outward appearance of tranquility, a sense of unease lingered in the air, like a shadow lurking just beyond the edges of perception.

In the aftermath of the fire that had ravaged the town square, the residents of Justice found themselves grappling with fear and suspicion. Whispers echoed through the streets, rumors swirling like leaves caught in a gust of wind. Some whispered of foul play, of hidden motives and dark conspiracies lurking beneath the surface. Others spoke of divine retribution, of a town cursed by its own sins and transgressions.

Among the townsfolk, there was no shortage of speculation as to the true cause of the fire. Some blamed it on careless negligence, while others pointed fingers at unseen enemies lurking in the shadows. But amidst the confusion and uncertainty, one thing was clear: the events of the previous night had shattered the fragile peace of Justice, leaving its residents on edge and uncertain of what the future might hold.

In the town square, a makeshift memorial had sprung up in honor of those who had lost their lives in the fire. Flowers and candles adorned the charred remains of the buildings, casting flickering shadows on the ground below. Mourners gathered around the memorial, their faces drawn and somber as they paid their respects to the fallen.

But even as they mourned, a sense of tension hung in the air, palpable and suffocating. The usual chatter and laughter that filled the town square had been replaced by a heavy silence, broken only by the occasional whispered conversation or furtive glance cast over a shoulder.

Among the mourners stood Sarah Thompson, her eyes red-rimmed with tears as she surveyed the scene before her. Guilt gnawed at her insides, a bitter taste in her mouth as she wrestled with the knowledge that she had been unable to save everyone from the fire. But even as she mourned the loss of life, a fire burned within her, fueled by a fierce determination to uncover the truth behind the tragedy that had befallen her town.

As the day wore on, the whispers grew louder, rumors spreading like wildfire through the streets of Justice. Some claimed to have seen shadowy figures lurking in the alleys at night, while others spoke of strange lights flickering in the darkness. Fear gripped the town like a vice, its tendrils creeping into every corner and crevice, leaving no one untouched.

But amidst the fear and uncertainty, a glimmer of hope flickered in the darkness. For Sarah Thompson and a handful of other brave souls, the events of the previous night had only strengthened their resolve to uncover the truth and bring those responsible to justice. And as they set out to unravel the mystery that had plunged their town into chaos, they knew that they would stop at nothing to see justice done, no matter the cost.

3

Unveiling Shadows

As night fell once again over the town of Justice, the streets grew quiet, shrouded in an eerie stillness broken only by the occasional whisper of the wind. In the dim light of the moon, shadows danced upon the cobblestones, casting strange and unsettling shapes upon the ground.

In the heart of the town, the imposing form of the town hall loomed over the square like a silent sentinel, its windows dark and foreboding. Inside, Mayor Ethan Blackwood sat alone in his office, the soft glow of lamplight casting long shadows across his face as he pored over a stack of papers spread out before him.

But despite the appearance of calm, a storm was brewing beneath the surface, threatening to engulf Justice in its fury. For hidden within the labyrinthine corridors of power that lurked within the town hall, a dark secret lay waiting to be uncovered, a secret that had the power to shake the very foundations of the town to its core.

As Mayor Blackwood sat lost in thought, a soft knock sounded at the door, interrupting his reverie. Frowning, he rose from his desk and crossed the room to open the door, revealing the figure of his loyal aide, Thomas Hawthorne, standing on the threshold.

"Sir, forgive the intrusion," Thomas began, his voice hushed with urgency, "but there's something you need to see."

Curiosity piqued, Mayor Blackwood followed Thomas out of the office and down a narrow corridor, their footsteps echoing softly in the silence. They emerged into a dimly lit chamber, its walls lined with shelves overflowing with dusty tomes and ancient artifacts.

In the center of the room stood a large oak table, upon which lay a tattered journal bound in faded leather. Thomas gestured towards it, his expression grave.

"I found this while going through some old records," he explained, his voice barely above a whisper. "It belonged to one of the town's founding families, but it seems to contain some rather... troubling entries."

Mayor Blackwood's eyes narrowed as he reached for the journal, flipping through its pages with growing unease. As he read, a cold knot formed in the pit of his stomach, for the words contained within revealed a dark and sinister truth about the town of Justice, one that had remained hidden for generations.

As the night wore on, Mayor Blackwood and Thomas delved deeper into the journal, their minds reeling with the implications of what they had discovered. For it seemed that the town's prosperity was built upon a foundation of lies and deceit, and those who had wielded power in the past had done so at a terrible cost.

But even as they grappled with the weight of this revelation, a shadowy figure lurked in the darkness, watching and waiting. For they knew that the secrets contained within the journal had the power to destroy everything Mayor

Blackwood had worked so hard to build, and they would stop at nothing to ensure that they remained buried forever.

And so, as the first light of dawn began to creep over the horizon, Mayor Blackwood and Thomas were left with a choice: to confront the darkness that lurked within the heart of Justice, or to turn away and risk losing everything they held dear. But whatever path they chose, one thing was certain: the shadows that had long haunted the town were beginning to stir, and Justice would never be the same again.

4

Echoes of the Past

In the dim light of dawn, the town of Justice stirred to life once more, its residents emerging from the shadows of the night to greet the new day with a mixture of hope and trepidation. But for Sarah Thompson, the events of the previous night lingered in her mind like a dark cloud, casting a pall over her thoughts as she went about her daily routine.

As she made her way through the bustling streets of Justice, Sarah couldn't shake the feeling that something was amiss, that there were secrets lurking beneath the surface of the town waiting to be uncovered. And as she passed by the charred remains of the buildings in the town square, the memories of the fire still fresh in her mind, she resolved to delve deeper into the mystery that had plunged her town into chaos.

Her first stop was the town library, a small but cozy building nestled in the heart of Justice. Pushing open the heavy oak door, Sarah stepped inside, the scent of old books and dust filling her nostrils as she made her way to the history section. She had a hunch that the answers she sought lay buried within the pages of the town's past, and she was determined to uncover them, no matter the cost.

For hours, Sarah poured over ancient tomes and faded manuscripts, her eyes scanning the pages for any clue that might shed light on the events that had transpired in Justice. And then, just as she was about to give up hope, she stumbled upon a dusty old journal tucked away in a forgotten corner of the library.

As she flipped through its pages, her heart quickened with excitement, for the journal contained the handwritten accounts of one of Justice's founding families, detailing their struggles and triumphs as they carved out a life for themselves in the untamed wilderness of the New World. But it was one particular entry that caught Sarah's eye, a passage written in a shaky hand that spoke of a dark secret hidden beneath the surface of Justice, a secret that had the power to destroy everything the town held dear.

With trembling hands, Sarah copied down the passage, her mind racing with possibilities as she tried to make sense of the cryptic words. It seemed that the town's prosperity was built upon a foundation of blood and betrayal, and those who had wielded power in the past had done so at a terrible cost.

But even as Sarah grappled with the implications of her discovery, a shadowy figure watched from the shadows, their eyes glittering with malice. They knew that Sarah was getting too close to the truth, and they would stop at nothing to see her silenced.

And so, as the sun dipped below the horizon and darkness descended once more upon the town of Justice, Sarah knew that she was treading on dangerous ground. But she also knew that she couldn't turn back now, not when the fate of her town hung in the balance. And with a steely resolve, she vowed to uncover the truth, no matter the cost.

5

A Gathering Storm

The town of Justice simmered with tension as whispers of Sarah Thompson's discoveries spread like wildfire through the streets. In the wake of her revelations, the once tranquil community found itself teetering on the brink of chaos, its residents grappling with fear and uncertainty as they wondered what other secrets lay hidden beneath the surface.

In the town square, a crowd had gathered, drawn by the promise of answers and the specter of impending danger. Among them stood Sarah, her heart pounding in her chest as she prepared to share her findings with the townsfolk. But as she stepped forward to speak, a voice rang out from the crowd, cutting through the murmurs and whispers like a knife.

It was Mayor Ethan Blackwood, his voice smooth and honeyed as he addressed the gathered throng. "My fellow citizens," he began, his words tinged with an air of authority, "I urge you not to heed the wild accusations of a misguided few. The prosperity of our town has always been built upon a foundation of honesty and integrity, and I assure you that there is no truth to these baseless claims."

But even as Mayor Blackwood spoke, a murmur of dissent rippled through the crowd, the townsfolk exchanging uneasy glances as they wondered who to believe. For Sarah's revelations had struck a nerve, stirring long-buried memories and casting doubt upon everything they thought they knew about their town and its history.

As the crowd began to disperse, Sarah felt a hand on her shoulder, turning to find herself face to face with Thomas Hawthorne, the mayor's loyal aide. "You've stirred up quite a hornet's nest, Miss Thompson," he said, his voice low and conspiratorial. "But be careful. There are those who will stop at nothing to protect their secrets, no matter the cost."

Sarah nodded solemnly, her mind whirling with possibilities as she pondered Thomas's words. For she knew that she was treading on dangerous ground, that the forces arrayed against her were powerful and ruthless. But she also knew that she couldn't turn back now, not when the fate of her town hung in the balance.

Determined to uncover the truth, Sarah set out to gather more evidence, enlisting the help of a handful of trusted allies who shared her desire for justice. Together, they combed through old records and interviewed townsfolk, piecing together a puzzle whose edges were shrouded in darkness.

But as they delved deeper into the mystery, they soon realized that they were not the only ones seeking answers. For lurking in the shadows, a shadowy figure watched their every move, their eyes glittering with malice as they plotted to silence Sarah and her allies once and for all.

And so, as the sun dipped below the horizon and darkness descended upon the town of Justice, Sarah knew that the storm was gathering, its fury poised to break upon the unsuspecting residents like a tidal wave. But she also knew that she would not rest until the truth was revealed, no matter the cost. For Justice demanded nothing less than absolute transparency, and Sarah was determined to see that justice was done, no matter what dangers lay ahead.

6

The Veil Lifts

As the moon hung low in the sky, casting its silvery glow over the town of Justice, a sense of unease settled over the residents like a heavy fog. In the wake of Sarah Thompson's revelations, the once peaceful community had become a tinderbox of suspicion and mistrust, its residents eyeing each other with wary glances as they wondered who among them could be trusted.

In the heart of the town, Mayor Ethan Blackwood sat alone in his office, the flickering light of a single candle casting long shadows across the walls. His brow furrowed in thought as he pondered the implications of Sarah's discoveries, a cold knot forming in the pit of his stomach as he realized that his carefully constructed facade was beginning to crumble around him.

But even as Mayor Blackwood wrestled with his own demons, a knock sounded at the door, jolting him from his reverie. Frowning, he rose from his desk and crossed the room to open the door, revealing the figure of Thomas Hawthorne standing on the threshold, his expression grave.

"Sir, we have a problem," Thomas began, his voice tight with tension. "Sarah Thompson and her allies are getting too close to the truth. We need to act, and we need to act now."

Mayor Blackwood's eyes narrowed at the mention of Sarah's name, his mind racing with possibilities as he considered his next move. For he knew that Sarah posed a threat to everything he had worked so hard to build, and he could not afford to let her unravel his carefully laid plans.

And so, with a steely resolve, Mayor Blackwood and Thomas set out to silence Sarah and her allies once and for all. They dispatched a group of hired thugs to confront them, their orders clear: eliminate anyone who stood in the way of their plans, no questions asked.

Meanwhile, Sarah and her allies continued their investigation, unaware of the danger that lurked just around the corner. As they combed through old records and pieced together clues, they felt a sense of urgency gnawing at their insides, a feeling that time was running out and that the truth was slipping through their fingers like grains of sand.

But even as they pressed forward, determined to see justice done, a shadowy figure watched their every move from the darkness, their eyes glittering with malice. They knew that Sarah was getting too close to the truth, and they would stop at nothing to see her silenced, even if it meant resorting to violence.

And so, as the night wore on and the tension in the air grew thicker with each passing moment, Sarah and her allies found themselves on a collision course with destiny, their fates hanging in the balance as they raced to uncover the truth before it was too late. But little did they know that the veil of secrecy that had long shrouded the town of Justice was about to be lifted, revealing the dark and sinister truth that lay hidden beneath the surface.

7

Into the Abyss

The night air hung heavy with anticipation as Sarah Thompson and her allies continued their investigation into the dark secrets of Justice. With each passing moment, the tension in the air seemed to thicken, as if the very atmosphere itself was holding its breath in anticipation of the coming storm.

In the heart of the town, Mayor Ethan Blackwood and his loyal aide, Thomas Hawthorne, watched from the shadows, their hearts filled with trepidation as they waited for word of their hired thugs' success. For they knew that Sarah and her allies posed a threat to everything they had worked so hard to build, and they could not afford to let them uncover the truth.

And then, as if on cue, the sound of footsteps echoed through the darkness, drawing closer with each passing moment. Mayor Blackwood's heart quickened with anticipation as he watched the approaching figures, his hand clenching into a fist as he prepared to strike.

But as the figures drew nearer, a sense of unease washed over Mayor Blackwood, for there was something in their eyes that sent a shiver down his spine, a glint of madness and cruelty that spoke of a darkness lurking within.

And then, with a sudden burst of violence, chaos erupted in the streets of Justice as Sarah and her allies found themselves ambushed by Mayor Blackwood's hired thugs. Blades flashed in the moonlight as they clashed with their assailants, the sounds of grunts and curses mingling with the clang of metal on metal as they fought for their lives.

But even as they battled against overwhelming odds, Sarah and her allies refused to back down, their determination unwavering as they pressed forward, driven by a fierce desire to see justice done. For they knew that they were fighting not just for themselves, but for the very soul of their town, and they would not rest until the truth was revealed.

As the fight raged on, a shadowy figure watched from the sidelines, their eyes glittering with malice as they reveled in the chaos unfolding before them. For they knew that Sarah and her allies were getting too close to the truth, and they would stop at nothing to see them silenced, even if it meant resorting to violence.

And so, as the night wore on and the streets ran red with blood, Sarah and her allies found themselves locked in a desperate struggle for survival, their every move shadowed by the specter of death. But amidst the chaos and carnage, a glimmer of hope flickered in the darkness, for they knew that they were not alone in their fight.

And as they fought side by side, their bonds strengthened by adversity, they vowed to see justice done, no matter the cost. For they knew that the road ahead would be long and treacherous, but they were determined to see it through to the end, even if it meant venturing into the abyss.

8

Rising from the Ashes

In the aftermath of the violent confrontation in the streets of Justice, the town lay in shambles, its once vibrant streets now silent and deserted. The echoes of the battle still lingered in the air, mingling with the acrid scent of smoke and blood that hung heavy over the town like a shroud.

Among the ruins, Sarah Thompson and her allies regrouped, their faces grim and determined as they surveyed the devastation that surrounded them. Though battered and bruised, their spirits remained unbroken, their resolve as strong as ever as they prepared to continue their fight for justice.

But as they picked through the rubble, searching for any sign of their assailants, a sense of unease settled over them like a dark cloud. For they knew that the forces aligned against them were powerful and ruthless, and that they would stop at nothing to see them silenced.

And then, just as they were about to give up hope, a figure emerged from the shadows, their face obscured by the darkness. At first, Sarah and her allies tensed, ready to defend themselves against yet another attack. But as the figure drew nearer, they realized with a start that it was none other than

Thomas Hawthorne, the loyal aide to Mayor Ethan Blackwood.

Breathless and disheveled, Thomas stumbled forward, his eyes wild with panic as he relayed a chilling message to Sarah and her allies. "They're coming," he gasped, his voice hoarse with fear. "Mayor Blackwood's men. They're coming for you, and they won't stop until they've silenced you for good."

With a sinking feeling in their hearts, Sarah and her allies knew that they had no choice but to flee. And so, with Thomas leading the way, they slipped through the streets of Justice like ghosts, their footsteps silent against the cobblestones as they sought refuge in the shadows.

But even as they fled, a sense of desperation gnawed at their insides, for they knew that they could not outrun their pursuers forever. And so, as they made their way through the darkened alleyways and deserted streets, they searched for a glimmer of hope amidst the darkness that threatened to consume them.

And then, just when all seemed lost, they stumbled upon a hidden refuge nestled in the heart of Justice, a secret sanctuary known only to a select few. With a sense of relief washing over them, Sarah and her allies slipped inside, the heavy oak door creaking shut behind them as they huddled together in the darkness, their hearts pounding in their chests as they waited for the storm to pass.

Outside, the streets of Justice lay silent and deserted, the town holding its breath as it waited for the inevitable confrontation that loomed on the horizon. But amidst the chaos and uncertainty, a glimmer of hope flickered in the darkness, for Sarah and her allies knew that they were not alone in their fight.

And as they prepared to face whatever challenges lay ahead, they vowed to rise from the ashes of their shattered town, stronger and more determined than ever before. For they knew that the road ahead would be long and treacherous, but they were ready to face whatever obstacles stood in their way, no matter the cost.

9

The Battle Lines Drawn

Inside the hidden refuge in the heart of Justice, Sarah Thompson and her allies huddled together, their breaths shallow and hearts pounding as they awaited the inevitable confrontation that loomed on the horizon. Outside, the town lay cloaked in darkness, its streets empty and silent save for the occasional whisper of the wind.

But amidst the stillness, a sense of tension hung in the air like a heavy fog, as if the very atmosphere itself was holding its breath in anticipation of the coming storm. For Sarah and her allies knew that they were not safe, that their enemies were closing in, their every move shadowed by the specter of death.

And then, just as they were about to lose hope, a glimmer of light appeared on the horizon, drawing closer with each passing moment. It was a group of townsfolk, their faces set in grim determination as they rallied to Sarah's cause, ready to stand by her side in the fight for justice.

With a sense of relief washing over them, Sarah and her allies prepared to face their enemies head-on, their spirits bolstered by the knowledge that they were not alone in their fight. For they knew that the battle ahead would be long and treacherous, but they were ready to face whatever challenges lay in their path, no matter the cost.

As dawn broke over the town of Justice, the streets came alive with activity, the air buzzing with anticipation as the residents prepared for the inevitable confrontation that loomed on the horizon. In the town square, a makeshift barricade had been erected, its defenses bolstered by the presence of Sarah and her allies, their faces set in grim determination as they prepared to defend their home against all who would seek to destroy it.

But even as they stood ready to face their enemies, a sense of unease gnawed at their insides, for they knew that the forces aligned against them were powerful and ruthless, and that the battle ahead would test their courage and resolve like never before.

And then, with a sudden burst of violence, chaos erupted in the streets of Justice as Mayor Ethan Blackwood's men descended upon the town, their weapons gleaming in the morning sun as they clashed with Sarah and her allies in a desperate struggle for control.

Blades flashed and arrows flew as the two sides battled for supremacy, the sounds of grunts and curses mingling with the clash of metal on metal as they fought tooth and nail for their lives. But amidst the chaos and carnage, a glimmer of hope flickered in the darkness, for Sarah and her allies knew that they were not alone in their fight.

With each passing moment, more townsfolk rallied to their cause, their numbers swelling as they joined the fray, their faces set in grim determination as they fought side by side with Sarah and her allies in the battle for justice.

And as the sun reached its zenith and the battle raged on into the afternoon, the streets of Justice ran red with blood, the town holding its breath as it waited to see who would emerge victorious from the crucible of war. But amidst the chaos and uncertainty, one thing was clear: the battle lines had been drawn, and there could be no turning back.

10

Dark Revelations

The sun hung low in the sky, casting long shadows over the bloodstained streets of Justice as the battle raged on into the evening. Sarah Thompson and her allies fought with all their might, their faces grim and determined as they clashed with Mayor Ethan Blackwood's men in a desperate struggle for control of the town.

But amidst the chaos and carnage, a sense of unease gnawed at Sarah's insides, for she knew that the true battle lay not on the streets, but within the hearts and minds of the townsfolk themselves. For too long, they had been kept in the dark, their lives governed by fear and ignorance, and Sarah knew that if they were to have any hope of winning the war, they would need to expose the truth for all to see.

With a steely resolve, Sarah rallied her allies to her side, their faces set in grim determination as they prepared to face the darkness head-on. Together, they combed through old records and pieced together clues, determined to uncover the truth behind the dark secrets that had long haunted their town.

And then, just when all seemed lost, they stumbled upon a hidden chamber buried deep beneath the town hall, its walls lined with shelves overflowing with dusty tomes and ancient artifacts. With a sense of trepidation, they delved into the chamber, their hearts pounding in their chests as they searched for answers amidst the shadows.

And then, just as they were about to give up hope, Sarah stumbled upon a tattered journal tucked away in a forgotten corner of the chamber. As she flipped through its pages, her heart quickened with excitement, for the journal contained the handwritten accounts of one of Justice's founding families, detailing their struggles and triumphs as they carved out a life for themselves in the untamed wilderness of the New World.

But it was one particular entry that caught Sarah's eye, a passage written in a shaky hand that spoke of a dark secret hidden beneath the surface of Justice, a secret that had the power to destroy everything the town held dear. With trembling hands, Sarah copied down the passage, her mind racing with possibilities as she tried to make sense of the cryptic words.

And then, just as she was about to share her discovery with her allies, a shadowy figure emerged from the darkness, their eyes glittering with malice as they moved to strike. With a cry of warning, Sarah pushed her allies out of harm's way, her heart pounding in her chest as she prepared to face her enemy alone.

But even as she stood ready to defend herself, a voice rang out from the darkness, cutting through the tension like a knife. It was Mayor Ethan Blackwood, his voice smooth and honeyed as he stepped forward to reveal the truth behind the dark secrets that had long haunted their town.

With a sense of shock and disbelief, Sarah listened as Mayor Blackwood revealed the depths of his deception, his words like poison as they dripped from his lips. For it seemed that the town's prosperity was built upon a foundation of lies and deceit, and those who had wielded power in the past had done so at a terrible cost.

And as the truth washed over her, Sarah knew that the battle ahead would be unlike any she had ever faced before. For the darkness that had long lurked within the heart of Justice had finally been exposed, and there could be no turning back.

11

The Final Stand

The revelation of Mayor Ethan Blackwood's deception hung heavy in the air, casting a pall over the hidden chamber beneath the town hall. Sarah Thompson and her allies stood frozen in shock, their minds reeling with the implications of his words.

But even as the truth sank in, a sense of determination burned bright within Sarah's heart. For she knew that the battle was far from over, and that they could not rest until justice was served and the darkness that had long plagued their town was vanquished once and for all.

With a steely resolve, Sarah turned to face Mayor Blackwood, her eyes ablaze with righteous fury as she prepared to confront him. "You may have deceived the people of Justice for far too long," she declared, her voice ringing with conviction, "but your reign of terror ends here and now."

Mayor Blackwood's lips curled into a cold smile, his eyes glinting with malice as he regarded Sarah and her allies. "You may have uncovered the truth," he said, his voice dripping with disdain, "but what good will it do you? The people of Justice are mine to control, and they will never believe the words of a mere handful of rebels."

But even as Mayor Blackwood spoke, a murmuring began to spread through the chamber, the townsfolk who had gathered to witness the confrontation exchanging uneasy glances as they listened to Sarah's words. For they knew that the truth could not be denied, and that the time had come for them to stand up and fight for their freedom.

With a rallying cry, Sarah and her allies charged forward, their hearts filled with determination as they faced off against Mayor Blackwood and his loyalists. Blades flashed in the dim light of the chamber, the sounds of clashing steel echoing off the stone walls as the two sides clashed in a desperate struggle for control.

But even as they fought, Sarah knew that victory would not come easily. For Mayor Blackwood was a cunning adversary, and he would stop at nothing to see his enemies vanquished. With each passing moment, the battle grew fiercer, the stakes higher, as the fate of Justice hung in the balance.

And then, just when all seemed lost, a glimmer of hope appeared on the horizon. It was the townsfolk of Justice, their faces set in grim determination as they rallied to Sarah's cause, their numbers swelling with each passing moment as they joined the fray.

With renewed vigor, Sarah and her allies pressed forward, their spirits bolstered by the knowledge that they were not alone in their fight. Together, they fought side by side, their bonds strengthened by adversity, as they faced down Mayor Blackwood and his loyalists in the final showdown for the soul of their town.

And as the battle raged on into the night, the streets of Justice ran red with blood, the sounds of clashing steel and desperate cries filling the air as the two sides clashed with all their might. But amidst the chaos and carnage, a sense of hope burned bright within Sarah's heart, for she knew that victory was within their grasp.

And then, with a final, decisive blow, Mayor Ethan Blackwood fell, his reign of terror coming to an end at last. With a cry of triumph, Sarah and her allies emerged victorious, their faces weary but their spirits soaring as they looked out over the town they had fought so hard to save.

For Justice had been redeemed, its darkest secrets laid bare for all to see. And as the sun rose over the horizon, casting its golden light upon the bloodstained streets, Sarah Thompson knew that the town she called home would never be the same again. But amidst the ruins of the past, a new dawn was rising, one filled with hope and promise for the future.

12

Rebuilding from the Ashes

The sun rose over the town of Justice, casting its warm rays upon the once-bloodstained streets now littered with debris and remnants of the fierce battle that had raged just hours before. The air was heavy with the scent of smoke and the echoes of conflict, yet amidst the destruction, a sense of newfound hope began to blossom.

Sarah Thompson stood amidst the rubble, her eyes sweeping over the scene before her. Despite the devastation, her heart swelled with pride at the sight of her fellow townsfolk emerging from their homes, ready to roll up their sleeves and begin the arduous task of rebuilding their beloved town.

With a determined spirit, Sarah set to work alongside her allies, their hands moving with purpose as they cleared away debris and salvaged what they could from the wreckage. The sound of hammers and saws filled the air as buildings began to rise from the ashes, their foundations strong and unwavering as a testament to the resilience of the people of Justice.

But even as they worked tirelessly to rebuild their town, a sense of unease lingered in the air, for they knew that the wounds inflicted by Mayor Ethan

Blackwood's reign of terror would not heal overnight. There were scars that ran deep, wounds that could not be easily erased, and they would need time to mend.

And then, just when all seemed lost, a glimmer of hope appeared on the horizon. It was Mayor Blackwood's former aides, Thomas Hawthorne among them, stepping forward to offer their assistance in the rebuilding efforts. With humility and remorse in their hearts, they pledged to atone for their past mistakes and work alongside Sarah and her allies to build a better future for Justice.

With a sense of cautious optimism, Sarah accepted their offer, knowing that true healing could only come through forgiveness and reconciliation. And as the days turned into weeks and the weeks into months, the town of Justice began to rise from the ashes, stronger and more united than ever before.

But amidst the rebuilding efforts, a shadowy figure lurked in the darkness, their eyes glittering with malice as they watched from the sidelines. For they knew that the wounds inflicted upon Justice ran deep, and that the scars left behind by Mayor Blackwood's reign of terror would not fade so easily.

And so, as the town of Justice began to heal, Sarah Thompson remained ever vigilant, knowing that the battle for justice was far from over. But amidst the uncertainty and the challenges that lay ahead, one thing was certain: the people of Justice would never again allow themselves to be ruled by fear and tyranny.

For they had fought too hard and sacrificed too much to let their town fall into darkness once more. And as they looked to the future with hope in their hearts, they knew that no matter what challenges lay ahead, they would face them together, as one united community, determined to build a brighter tomorrow for themselves and for generations to come.